Biographies

Vasco

DA GAMA

by Kathleen McFarren

Consultant:

John P. Boubel, Ph.D.

History Professor, Bethany Lutheran College

Mankato, Minnesota

Capstone *press*

Mankato, Minnesota

Fact Finders is published by Capstone Press
151 Good Counsel Drive, P.O. Box 669, Mankato, Minnesota 56002
www.capstonepress.com

Library of Congress Cataloging-in-Publication Data
McFarren, Kathleen.
    Vasco da Gama / by Kathleen McFarren.
    p. cm.—(Fact finders. Biographies)
    Summary: An introduction to the life of fifteenth-century Portuguese explorer Vasco
da Gama, who strengthened his nation's power by expanding trade routes to India.
    Includes bibliographical references (p. 31) and index.
    ISBN 0-7368-2491-X (hardcover)
    1. Gama, Vasco da, 1469–1524—Travel—Juvenile literature. 2. Explorers—Portugal—
Biography—Juvenile literature. 3. Discoveries in geography—Portuguese—Juvenile
literature. [1. Gama, Vasco da, 1469–1524. 2. Explorers.] I. Title. II. Series.
G286.G2M44 2004
910'.92—dc22   2003015382

Editorial Credits

Roberta Schmidt, editor; Juliette Peters, designer; Linda Clavel and Heather Kindseth,
    illustrators; Deirdre Barton and Wanda Winch, photo researchers; Eric Kudalis,
    product planning editor

Photo Credits

Art Resource, NY/Giraudon, 17
Bartrick Antique Prints & Maps, 16
Corbis/Bettmann, 9, 12–13; Eye Ubiquitous/Bennett Dean, 20–21; Tony Arruza, 6–7
Corbis Sygma/John Van Hasselt, 15
Getty Images/Hulton Archive, cover, 11; Kean Collection, 24–25; Roger Viollet, 1
Mary Evans Picture Library, 4–5, 14, 23
North Wind Picture Archives, 10, 22
Stock Montage Inc., 18–19

1 2 3 4 5 6 09 08 07 06 05 04

Table of Contents

Chapter 1

Calicut

On May 20, 1498, three large ships sailed near the busy city of Calicut. The men on the ships could see into the city's **harbor**. They saw many kinds of **spices** and trade goods. The men knew they had finally reached India.

The **voyage** was long and difficult. The men left Portugal almost a year earlier. Their captain led them all the way to the southern tip of Africa. They then sailed up the east side of the continent. No European had sailed there before. Along the way, the men met new people. They also fought some battles. But their voyage was finally over.

This 1600s engraving shows Portuguese traders in Calicut, India.

After landing in India, the captain ordered his men to set up a large stone marker on the shore. The captain's name was Vasco da Gama. The marker showed that they were the first Europeans to sail to India.

Chapter 2

A Portuguese Beginning

Vasco da Gama was born in Sines, Portugal, around 1469. Sines lies in southern Portugal along the Atlantic Ocean. Da Gama's father was the **governor** of Sines.

Little is known about da Gama's childhood. He was the youngest of three sons. Da Gama grew up learning about sailing and exploring. He also studied math and navigation.

When da Gama was 15 years old, he joined short trading voyages to Africa. Da Gama learned how to be a sailor and a good leader.

DOM VASCO DA GAMA
1469 - 1524

DESCOBRIDOR E ALMIRANTE DO MAR DA INDIA
R CONDE DA VIDIGUEIRA
VICE - REI DA INDIA

"...AQUELLE ILLUSTRE GAMA
QUE PARA SI DE ENEAS TOMA A FAMA."
CAMÕES, LUZ, I - 12

A statue of da Gama
stands in Sines, Portugal.

Chapter 3

The Urge to Explore

Da Gama grew up during an important time in Portugal's history. In the early 1400s, Europeans did not know much about the world beyond Europe. Around 1420, Prince Henry of Portugal started to hire sailors to **explore** the west coast of Africa. Over the next 40 years, the Portuguese pushed farther south into unknown areas. By the late 1400s, the Portuguese were known as the best **navigators** and mapmakers in Europe.

Prince Henry sent sailors
to explore the unknown
west coast of Africa.

▲ For hundreds of years, most trade with Asia was done overland.

Eastern Trade

The Portuguese had an important reason for their exploration. They wanted to find a water route to India, China, and Japan. These countries had **silk** and spices that Europe did not have. Europeans wanted to trade for these items.

Trading between Europe and Asia was hard. Arabs lived between Europe and Asia. They controlled the trade. They made Europeans pay high prices for goods. The Europeans wanted to trade directly with India, China, and Japan. Many Europeans looked for ways to reach Asia.

Prince Henry believed India could be reached by sea. He only had to find a way around Africa. By the time Prince Henry died in 1460, his explorers had sailed down about one-third of the African coast.

The Tip of Africa

In 1488, Portuguese explorer Bartolomeu Dias reached the southern tip of Africa. The Portuguese then knew that India could be reached by sea.

Almost 10 years passed before Portugal was ready to send men on the long voyage to India. King Manuel asked Vasco da Gama to lead them.

King Manuel of Portugal asked da Gama to sail to India.

Chapter 4

The Voyage

Da Gama set sail from Lisbon, Portugal, on July 8, 1497. He had four ships and at least 160 men. Da Gama sailed aboard the *São Gabriel*. His brother Paulo **commanded** the *São Rafael*. One of King Manuel's relatives was in charge of the *Berrio*. The fourth ship carried food and supplies.

Da Gama and his men carried enough food and supplies to last three years. They also brought cloth, hats, bells, and other trinkets to trade with the people they met.

Lisbon was a major port city in Portugal.

Down the West Coast

The **fleet** sailed down the west coast of Africa. Near the equator, da Gama steered his ships far out into the ocean. There, the ships did not have to fight the winds and ocean currents. After a few months, the ships headed back toward Africa.

Da Gama's ships made a wide arc into the Atlantic Ocean.

14

On November 7, the ships landed at St. Helena Bay. Da Gama and his men stayed at St. Helena Bay for nine days. They fixed leaks in the ships. They also traded with the African people they met there.

Around the Cape

On November 22, the ships rounded the Cape of Good Hope. Da Gama and his men had used many supplies. They did not need the big supply ship anymore. They burned it so no one else could use it. A few weeks later, they passed the farthest point Dias had reached. They were in unknown waters.

The supply ship was burned ▼ after it was no longer needed.

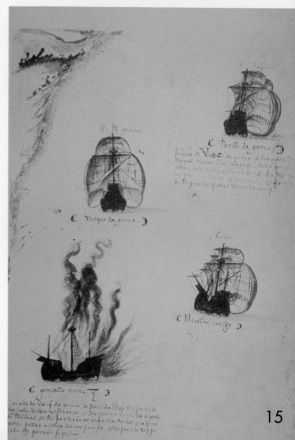

▲ Da Gama met many African people. One group was the Hottentots.

Up the East Coast

Da Gama and his men sailed up the east coast of Africa. They met and traded with more African people.

On March 2, 1498, da Gama's fleet reached Mozambique. This city was very rich. Mozambique had gold, silver, and spices.

Many Arab traders lived in Mozambique. They did not like da Gama's cheap trinkets. They refused to trade with the Portuguese.

Da Gama became angry at the Arabs. As he left Mozambique, he fired cannons at the town. He took some men as **prisoners**.

Ibn Majid (pointing)
made the trip to
Calicut much easier
▼ and faster.

On April 15, da Gama's fleet stopped in Malindi. The ruler there agreed to trade with the Portuguese. He gave them food and spices. He also sent the Arab navigator Ahmad ibn Majid to help them reach India.

Ibn Majid guided da Gama's ships across the Indian Ocean in 23 days. They reached Calicut, India, on May 20, 1498.

Chapter 5

India

Da Gama and his men were amazed by the great riches in Calicut. The city was full of gold jewelry, pearls, rubies, and other precious stones. The men also saw many silks and spices.

Eight days after reaching Calicut, da Gama met the ruler of the city. The ruler was called the *zamorin*. Da Gama told the *zamorin* that Portugal wanted to be friends with India. The Portuguese wanted to trade for spices and jewels.

Da Gama tried to convince the *zamorin* to trade with him.

The *zamorin* was not sure he wanted to trade with the Portuguese. They only had cheap cloth and trinkets. These items were not fair trade for spices and jewels. The Arab traders also told the *zamorin* not to trade with the Portuguese.

The *zamorin* finally agreed to sell food to the Portuguese. He would not trade spices and jewels until they brought gold and silver.

Da Gama and his men did not get the riches they expected. But a few of the men traded in the Calicut markets. They got some jewels and spices.

The Portuguese left Calicut at the end of August. They sailed north to find better trade. But no one wanted to trade with them. In mid-October, da Gama turned his ships back toward Portugal.

India's markets still have many of the same spices that da Gama and his men saw.

Back to Portugal

The trip home was difficult. Da Gama did not have ibn Majid to guide him. It took da Gama three months to get back to Africa. The men ran out of food and fresh water. Many men became sick, and some died.

The Portuguese reached Malindi on January 7, 1499. The ruler there gave them meat, fruit, and other goods.

This map shows what Europeans thought Africa looked like in 1500.

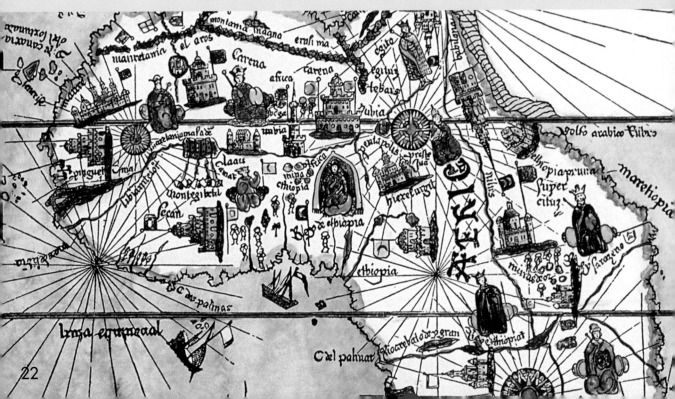

Da Gama did not have enough men to sail all three ships back to Portugal. On January 11, the men emptied the *São Rafael* and destroyed it.

On March 20, the *São Gabriel* and *Berrio* sailed past the Cape of Good Hope again. A few weeks later, they ran into a big storm. The ships lost sight of each other.

The ships sailed alone back to Portugal. The *Berrio* reached Lisbon on July 10. Da Gama and the *São Gabriel* got home in early September. Only 55 of da Gama's 160 men survived the trip.

FACT!

Many of da Gama's men had scurvy. People get this disease when they do not eat enough fruits and vegetables. Their skin turns yellow, their arms and legs swell up, and their teeth rot.

When da Gama returned to Portugal, he was honored by ▼ a visit from King Manuel.

Chapter 6

After the Voyage

Da Gama was welcomed in Portugal as a great hero. King Manuel gave him money, a house, and the title Admiral of the Indian Seas.

In 1502, da Gama went back to India to make trade agreements with the rulers there. He and his men fought the Arab traders and killed hundreds of people. They helped destroy the Arab trade. Da Gama then returned to Portugal.

In 1524, the king of Portugal sent da Gama back to India. The king made him the ruler of a **colony** there. But da Gama did not rule the colony very long. He became sick. Da Gama died on December 24, 1524.

Da Gama helped fight the Arabs
and take over the trade in India.

Lasting Impact

Da Gama brought riches and fame to himself and his country. He helped take the trade away from the Arabs who had controlled it for more than 500 years. The Portuguese took over the trade. They built trading colonies in many parts of the world. For the next 200 years, Portugal was one of the most powerful countries in Europe.

Da Gama's voyage showed that Europeans could sail around Africa and reach India. It also helped Europeans learn about other countries and people. Da Gama's voyage opened the world to new possibilities.

F A C T !

Da Gama's trip to India was the longest sea voyage in the history of the world up to that time. He and his men traveled about 27,000 miles (43,450 kilometers). They sailed four times as far as Christopher Columbus did in 1492.

The First Voyage of Vasco da Gama, 1497–1499

EUROPE

Portugal
● Lisbon

ASIA

AFRICA

● Calicut

EQUATOR

Malindi ●

INDIAN OCEAN

ATLANTIC OCEAN

Mozambique ●

St. Helena Bay

Cape of Good Hope

N
W   E
S

0	500	1,000 miles

0	1,000 kilometers

LEGEND
- ◄—— 1497–1498
- ◄—— 1498–1499
- ● City
- ------- Modern country boundary

Fast Facts

- Da Gama grew up in Portugal. He learned how to be a sailor and a good leader.

- Because of Prince Henry, the Portuguese learned much about navigating and the west coast of Africa.

- King Manuel sent da Gama to sail around Africa to reach India.

- On the way to India in 1497, da Gama and his men sailed far into the Atlantic Ocean. They did not see land for 13 weeks. Until this time, no one had ever sailed so long without seeing land.

- Da Gama met African people and Arabs on his voyage.

- India had great riches of jewels, spices, and silk.

- Da Gama helped make Portugal one of the richest countries in Europe.

Time Line

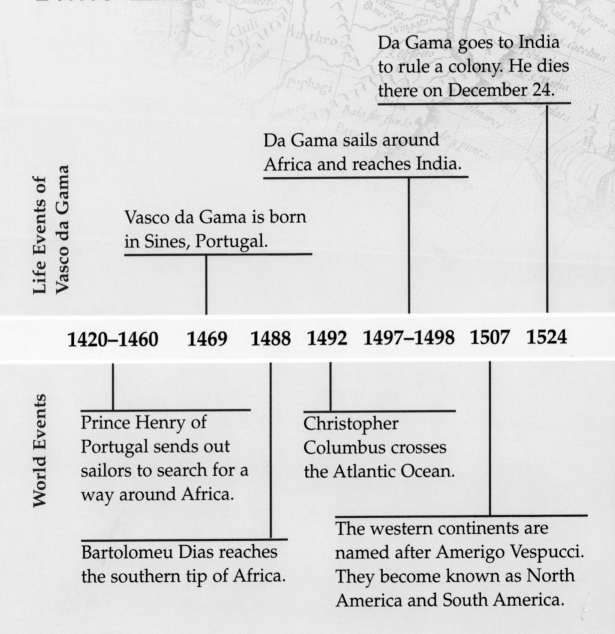

Life Events of Vasco da Gama

Da Gama goes to India to rule a colony. He dies there on December 24.

Da Gama sails around Africa and reaches India.

Vasco da Gama is born in Sines, Portugal.

1420–1460   1469   1488   1492   1497–1498   1507   1524

World Events

Prince Henry of Portugal sends out sailors to search for a way around Africa.

Christopher Columbus crosses the Atlantic Ocean.

Bartolomeu Dias reaches the southern tip of Africa.

The western continents are named after Amerigo Vespucci. They become known as North America and South America.

Glossary

colony (KOL-uh-nee)—an area that has been settled by people from another country; a colony is ruled by another country.

command (kuh-MAND)—to have control over something

explore (ek-SPLOR)—to travel to find out what a place is like

fleet (FLEET)—a group of ships that sail together

governor (GUHV-urn-ur)—a person who controls a country or state

harbor (HAR-bur)—a place where ships shelter or unload their cargo

navigator (NAV-uh-gay-tuhr)—a person who uses maps, compasses, and the stars to guide a ship

prisoner (PRIZ-uhn-ur)—a person who is held by force

silk (SILK)—a soft, shiny material made from fibers produced by a silkworm; silk is often made into clothing.

spice (SPISSE)—something used to flavor foods

voyage (VOI-ij)—a long journey

Internet Sites

FactHound offers a safe, fun way to find Internet sites related to this book. All of the sites on FactHound have been researched by our staff.

Here's how:
1. Visit *www.facthound.com*
2. Type in this special code **073682491X** for age-appropriate sites. Or enter a search word related to this book for a more general search.
3. Click on the **Fetch It** button.

FactHound will fetch the best sites for you!

Read More

Doak, Robin S. *Da Gama: Vasco da Gama Sails around the Cape of Good Hope.* Exploring the World. Minneapolis: Compass Point Books, 2002.

Gallagher, Jim. *Vasco da Gama and the Portuguese Explorers.* Explorers of New Worlds. Philadelphia: Chelsea House, 2000.

Goodman, Joan Elizabeth. *A Long and Uncertain Journey: The 27,000 Mile Voyage of Vasco da Gama.* A Great Explorers Book. New York: Mikaya Press, 2001.

Larkin, Tanya. *Vasco da Gama.* Famous Explorers. New York: PowerKids Press, 2001.

Index